Draw Along With Silver Matilda

The 'Get to Know Me' series is made up of resources aimed at children with additional needs. Developed by child psychologist Dr Louise Lightfoot and illustrated by Catherine Hicks, the series includes activities specific to anxiety, depression and Obsessive Compulsive Disorder (OCD). This book, *Draw Along With Silver Matilda*, is an activity-based picture book story, in which individual children are encouraged to interact with the story in a creative way – through writing, drawing, scrap booking, collage, activities etc.

Active engagement helps children to understand and process information, and aids long-term recall. It has been designed to support the individual child and encourage an empathetic and inclusive environment. In this book, we meet Silver Matilda, a bird with silver feathers known for her beauty and graceful flight. The story follows Matilda as she loses her bright feathers and, ashamed, hides away from the world until one day an owl comes and sits with her. The owl shows Matilda empathy and stays with her whilst she recovers and watches as she becomes stronger through her experience.

This book was written with children with depression in mind, providing an opportunity to relate to Matilda's thoughts, feelings, behaviours and experiences. However, children with a range of needs may benefit from the story. The book is written in a narrative style, so it does not use diagnostic labels and is not intended for this purpose. Instead the focus is on creating a common language which children can understand and use to make sense of how they are feeling.

A practitioner guidebook is also available (ISBN 978-0-8153-4943-3).

Dr Louise Lightfoot is an Educational and Child Psychologist working with children and young people aged 0–25. She holds a BA in Educational Studies, MEd in the Psychology of Education and doctorate in Educational and Child Psychology. Louise has worked in a variety of settings ranging from mainstream schools to secure units and psychiatric facilities, and has a special interest in working to empower at risk or 'hard to reach' groups. As a person who suffers with Ehlers Danlos, stroke and dyslexia, she has a first-hand understanding of the frustrations and difficulties that accompany a specific physical or learning difficulty. Louise currently works as an HCPC registered Independent Psychologist. If you would like to discuss working with her, please contact Louise at: louise.lightfoot@hotmail.co.uk.

Catherine Hicks is an East Yorkshire artist, illustrator, wife and mother. She spent 13 years as a Registered Veterinary Nurse before injury and chronic illnesses led to her creative hobby becoming therapy. When Catherine and Louise were introduced, it was obvious they were kindred spirits and from there the Get to Know Me Series was born.

GET TO KNOW ME SERIES

Series author: Dr Louise Lightfoot
Illustrated by: Catherine Hicks

The **'Get to Know Me'** series is a series of resources aimed at children with SEN or EBD and the professionals who support them in the mainstream primary classroom. Each resource concentrates on a different condition and comprises of three titles, available separately.

A **traditional children's picture book** – designed to support the individual child but also to be used in whole class teaching, to encourage an empathetic and inclusive environment.

An **interactive workbook**. This is a workbook version of the story in which individual children are encouraged to interact with the story in a creative way – through writing, drawing, scrap booking, collage, activities etc. (templates and cut outs will be made available online). Children are more likely to understand and process information if they have had to actively engage with it. The workbook will aid long-term recall and increase the level of understanding.

A **practitioner guide** created for key adults (teachers, therapists and parents) by a child psychologist, with activities specific to each condition. These activities will link to the books and offer practical tools and strategies to support the child and those around them in addition to the information specific to the condition to improve understanding of a child's needs to promote empathy and acceptance.

https://www.routledge.com/Get-To-Know-Me/book-series/GKM

Books included in this series:

Set 1 Get to Know Me: Anxiety
Available as a set and individual books

Book 1
Supporting Children with Anxiety to Understand and Celebrate Difference
A Get to Know Me Workbook and Guide for Parents and Practitioners
PB 978-0-8153-4941-9
eBook 978-1-351-16492-4

Book 2
Sammy Sloth
Get to Know Me: Anxiety
PB 978-0-8153-4953-2
eBook 978-1-351-16452-8

Book 3
Draw Along With Sammy Sloth
Get to Know Me: Anxiety
PB 978-0-8153-4942-6
eBook 978-1-351-16484-9

Set 2 Get to Know Me: Depression
Available as a set and individual books

Book 1
Supporting Children with Depression to Understand and Celebrate Difference
A Get to Know Me Workbook and Guide for Parents and Practitioners
PB 978-0-8153-4943-3
eBook 978-1-351-16480-1

Book 2
Silver Matilda
Get to Know Me: Depression
PB 978-0-8153-4945-7
eBook 978-1-351-16476-4

Book 3
Draw Along With Silver Matilda
Get to Know Me: Depression
PB 978-0-8153-4946-4
eBook 978-1-351-16472-6

Set 3 Get to Know Me: OCD
Available as a set and individual books

Book 1
Supporting Children with OCD to Understand and Celebrate Difference
A Get to Know Me Workbook and Guide for Parents and Practitioners
PB 978-0-8153-4948-8
eBook 978-1-351-16468-9

Book 2
Tidy Tim
Get to Know Me: OCD
PB 978-0-8153-4950-1
eBook 978-1-351-16460-3

Book 3
Draw Along With Tidy Tim
Get to Know Me: OCD
PB 978-0-8153-4951-8
eBook 978-1-351-16456-6

DRAW
ALONG WITH SILVER MATILDA

GET TO KNOW ME: DEPRESSION

DRAW YOUR OWN PICTURES FOR THE SILVER MATILDA STORY

DR LOUISE LIGHTFOOT

ILLUSTRATED BY CATHERINE HICKS

Routledge
Taylor & Francis Group

LONDON AND NEW YORK

First published 2020
by Routledge
2 Park Square, Milton Park, Abingdon, Oxon OX14 4RN

and by Routledge
52 Vanderbilt Avenue, New York, NY 10017

Routledge is an imprint of the Taylor & Francis Group, an informa business

British Library Cataloguing-in-Publication Data
A catalogue record for this book is available from the British Library

Library of Congress Cataloging-in-Publication Data
A catalog record has been requested for this book

ISBN: 978-0-8153-4946-4 (pbk)
ISBN: 978-1-351-16472-6 (ebk)

Typeset in Stone Informal
by Apex CoVantage, LLC

CONTENTS

WORK BOOK INSTRUCTIONS FOR PRACTITIONERS, PARENTS AND CARERS

The work book or draw along booklet can be useful in engaging children with poor literacy or a perceived dislike of formal 'work'. Often students with poor literacy, or those who struggle with comprehension, are not readily engaged in stories that may be of therapeutic value to them. Some children appear to read well but without additional prompts, may not understand the story or how it may relate to others/themselves. Often children will read with a focus on speed rather than on understanding and will look to the pictures for information when asked questions about what they have just read.

In taking away the pictures, this forces children to be active in their engagement with the story itself as they cannot rely on images to support their understanding. By asking pupils to draw (or colour pre-drawn images dependent on ability) images that correspond to the given text, this not only consolidates their understanding of the story but helps to engage the child in a creative process. Some children are more readily engaged in a task in which they can take ownership due their participation. They are able to create their own book which can represent their abilities when applied, high light any specific skills and act as a reminder of what they can achieve, especially if this surpasses their own expectations.

The booklet should be read with the support of a suitably skilled adult who has an understanding of the child's literacy abilities. If the child is able to read the story they should be encouraged to do so and to draw on each page a corresponding image. For able or confident pupils, they may be able to draw the complete image using pens/crayons complete with facial features depicting the mood and tone of the scene. Others may need more support and may colour, cut and stick in pre-drawn images and draw facial expressions with prompting from an adult or through choosing a facial expression from a given selection. Some children may be hesitant to draw but have great ideas and may ask an adult to draw their vision or use a computer to search for suitable images. However the book is completed, what matters is that all work is child-led and that their work is treated in a non-judgemental and positive manner. The adult should reassure the child that there is no right or wrong way to approach the task

The adult should gauge how appropriate it is to use the follow up questions provided (this may depend on verbal skills, confidence and trust/rapport) and if appropriate, the adult may decide to explore in depth a particular section of the story for example 'asking for help' if this is pertinent to the child's behaviour. In such a case they may decide to use the provided activities that are linked to each section of the story. An older or more able child might go through the book drawing each picture, discussing relevant topics and completing every additional activity. For some children, this process may be too much emotionally/beyond their attention span. The length of each session, the adult chosen to support the child and timing of the session are all factors that will contribute to the success of the work.

Adults engaging in such work should be suitably supported. Best practice is to offer supervision to them by an appropriate adult in recognition of the emotionally challenging nature of this delicate and potentially stressful work. Adults are encouraged to reflect on each session and to note useful insights; for example, can the child infer the characters emotions during a scene? Can they represent this through facial expression? Body language? Use of colour? How can any such observations be supported in the future?

The child is able to keep/refer back to their book and should be encouraged to take ownership of it in order to encourage engagement and improve self-esteem.

There once was bird
She was awesome and bright,
You might think her a star
If you saw her at night.

QUESTIONS: Matilda is very outgoing? Are you outgoing or shy?

Her name was Matilda,
And everyone knew
Of this beautiful bird
And all she could do.

Her eyes were like diamonds
That glistened and shone,
With a waterfall tail
That flowed on and on.

QUESTION: What are Matilda eyes like? Ask whoever is the youngest player to close their eyes and name the colour of the reader's eyes without peaking!

She danced on the clouds
And breezed through the sky;
She swirled and she twirled
And she fluttered on by.

You could not forget her
Once you'd seen her go by
You could only be dazzled
As she'd brighten the sky

QUESTIONS: Describe three ways Matilda moved when she was at her best. How do you move? Are you graceful like Matilda?

She bathed in the sunlight
On a bright summer's day,
Preening her feathers
Shining silvery grey.

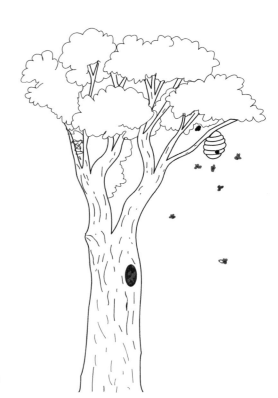

QUESTION: *What colour is your hair? Draw a picture*

She noticed a feather
Fall down to the floor;
She scrambled in panic
Afraid to see more.

And tears filled her eyes
As she looked all around
At the glistening trail
That littered the ground.

QUESTIONS: *What did Matilda lose? Have you ever lost anything important to you?*

And that's how it started;
On that very day
Matilda could feel herself
Fading away.

QUESTION: *Why do you think losing her feathers made Matilda so sad?*
Draw discuss with an adult

She didn't feel bright
Now she felt very small;
Now she didn't feel a bit like
Matilda at all.

So she sat in a huddle
Trying to hide in her wings;
Away from the world
And all troubling things.

But now all her feathers
Had fallen away,
She was no longer silver
She only felt grey.

QUESTION: Have you ever felt sad and alone? Draw or discuss with an adult

So she sat all alone
For the longest of whiles,
And felt far away
From a world full of smiles.

Then, all of a sudden,
She heard a voice say,
"Hello there Matilda
Are you hiding away?"

She felt so embarrassed;
"Please close your eyes,
I'm Silver Matilda,
the Queen of the skies.

QUESTION: *How did Matilda feel when someone saw her?*

"You can't see me like this
I'm broken and small.
I've lost all my feathers
Now I'm nothing at all."

"I'm Owen," said the owl
Who sat down by her side.
"Well, I see a bird
Who is hurting inside.

QUESTIONS: Was Owen put off by Matilda's appearance? Look at the words she describes to portray herself and find three which make her sound like a monster. How would you feel if you heard someone describing someone you loved like this?

"Don't feel afraid,
As from time to time
We all feel alone
And we might lose our shine.

"So we might need a friend
To help us find light,
Or simply to be there
As long as it's night."

QUESTION: Did Owen tell Matilda she was wrong or stupid this way?

And as the time passed
The owl didn't go,
He sat by her side
Until there was snow.

QUESTIONS: How long did the owl stay with Matilda?
How do you know?

And the world filled with colour
And was no longer grey,
She felt herself change
And night turned to day.

Her heart filled with love
Knowing someone did care,
Though she didn't look up
She knew Owen was there.

QUESTION: Would you have stayed there with Matilda for all of that time?

And that's when she noticed
Feathers starting to sprout,
All this time she'd been hiding
It was time to come out.

*QUESTION: What season was it now? Draw or discuss
with an adult*

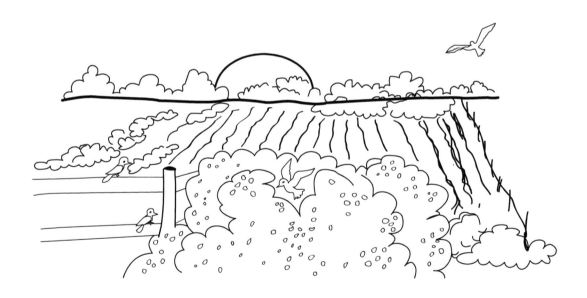

So she pulled back her wings
And saw friendly eyes,
And then her reflection
Oh what a surprise!

QUESTION: What was the first thing Matilda saw when she opened her eyes?

She couldn't believe it,
It gave her a fright.
She looked like Matilda
But now she was bright.

QUESTION: How have you overcome difficult times in the past?

And the owl had helped
Re-light the spark,
And saw her shine
When she felt only dark.

QUESTIONS: How had Owen helped Matilda? Do you think you have help someone when they are feeling sad?

And her heart was changed forever
By the kindness of another
Who brought her back from sadness
And helped her to recover.

She glimmered and shimmered,
Such a figure to behold,
She was no longer silver,
Now Matilda, she was gold.

QUESTIONS: What colour was Matilda at the end on the book? Do you think she had changed going through the process? Draw or discuss with an adult.

Colour, cut and stick pictures – use these however you like!